VITA & VIRGINIA

A Play

by Eileen Atkins

Adapted from the correspondence between
Virginia Woolf and Vita Sackville-West

D1303179

SAMUEL FRENCH

samuelfrench.co.uk

FOR AMATEUR PRODUCTION ENQUIRIES

UNITED KINGDOM AND WORLD
EXCLUDING NORTH AMERICA
plays@samuelfrench.co.uk
020 7255 4302/01

Each title is subject to availability from Samuel French, depending upon country of performance.

THINKING ABOUT PERFORMING A SHOW?

There are thousands of plays and musicals available to perform from Samuel French right now, and applying for a licence is easier and more affordable than you might think

---

From classic plays to brand new musicals, from monologues to epic dramas, there are shows for everyone.

Plays and musicals are protected by copyright law so if you want to perform them, the first thing you'll need is a licence. This simple process helps support the playwright by ensuring they get paid for their work, and means that you'll have the documents you need to stage the show in public.

Not all our shows are available to perform all the time, so it's important to check and apply for a licence before you start rehearsals or commit to doing the show.

LEARN MORE & FIND THOUSANDS OF SHOWS

Browse our full range of plays and musicals and find out more about how to license a show

www.samuelfrench.co.uk/perform

Talk to the friendly experts in our Licensing team for advice on choosing a show, and help with licensing

plays@samuelfrench.co.uk   020 7387 9373

Acting Editions

BORN TO PERFORM

Playscripts designed from the ground up to work the way you do in rehearsal, performance and study

---

Larger, clearer text for easier reading

Wider margins for notes

Performance features such as character and props lists, sound and lighting cues, and more

---

+ CHOOSE A SIZE AND STYLE TO SUIT YOU

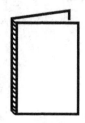

STANDARD EDITION

Our regular paperback book at our regular size

SPIRAL-BOUND EDITION

The same size as the Standard Edition, but with a sturdy, easy-to-fold, easy-to-hold spiral-bound spine

LARGE EDITION

A4 size and spiral bound, with larger text and a blank page for notes opposite every page of text. Perfect for technical and directing use

---

ABOUT THE AUTHOR

Dame Eileen June Atkins, DBE was born 16 June 1934. An English actress and occasional screenwriter. She has worked in the theatre, film, and television consistently since 1953. She has won several Major acting awards including three Olivier's, one BAFTA and one Emmy. She was appointed Commander of the Order of the British Empire (CBE) in 1990 and Dame Commander of the Order of the British Empire (DBE) in 2001.

AUTHOR'S NOTE

The issue of a licence to perform this play requires that any advertising or publicity material (including programmes) must include the following credit whenever the title of the play appears:

VITA & VIRGINIA
by Eileen Atkins

Adapted from correspondence between
Virginia Woolf and Vita Sackville-West

MUSIC USE NOTE

Licensees are solely responsible for obtaining formal written permission from copyright owners to use copyrighted music in the performance of this play and are strongly cautioned to do so. If no such permission is obtained by the licensee, then the licensee must use only original music that the licensee owns and controls. Licensees are solely responsible and liable for all music clearances and shall indemnify the copyright owners of the play(s) and their licensing agent, Samuel French, against any costs, expenses, losses and liabilities arising from the use of music by licensees. Please contact the appropriate music licensing authority in your territory for the rights to any incidental music.

IMPORTANT BILLING AND CREDIT REQUIREMENTS

If you have obtained performance rights to this title, please refer to your licensing agreement for important billing and credit requirements.

VITA AND VIRGINIA

First presented in the Minerva Studio, Chichester Festival Theatre, on 8th September 1992, with the following cast:

VITA SACKVILLE- WEST	Penelope Wilton
VIRGINIA WOOLF	Eileen Atkins

Directed by Patrick Garland
Designed by Lucy Hall

This production was subsequently presented by Robert Fox Limited and Lewis Allen at the Ambassadors Theatre, London, on 1st October 1993 with the same cast.

It was presented by Lewis Allen, Robert Fox Ltd, Julian Schlossberg with Mitchell Maxwell and Alan J. Schuster at the Union Square Theatre, New York, on 21st November, 1994, with the following cast:

VITA SACKVILLE-WEST	Vanessa Redgrave
VIRGINIA WOOLF	Eileen Atkins

Directed by Zoe Caldwell
Sets by Ben Edwards
Costumes by Jane Greenwood

ACKNOWLEDGEMENT

Eileen Atkins would like to thank Nigel Nicolson and Olivia and Quentin Bell without whose co-operation this production would not have been possible.

New York, June 1995

ACT I

This piece should be played as one long conversation except where it is indicated that the characters speak to the audience.

The lights come up.

VITA *(to the audience)* I simply adore Virginia Woolf and so would you, I met her last night at a party. She is utterly unaffected, nothing planned or self-conscious. She is both detached and human, silent till she wants to say something and then says it supremely well. She dresses quite atrociously. Last night she was wearing orange woollen stockings and had pinned together her silk rags with a gold brooch. She is quite old. I've rarely taken such a fancy to anyone and I think she likes me.

VIRGINIA *(to the audience)* I'm too muzzy-headed to make out anything. This is partly the result of dining to meet Mr and Mrs Harold Nicolson last night at Clive Bell's. She the lovely, gifted, aristocratic Vita Sackville-West—not much to my severer taste—florid, moustached, parakeet-coloured, with all the supple ease of the aristocracy but not the wit of the artist. She has her hand on all the ropes, makes me feel virgin-shy and schoolgirlish. Yet after dinner I rapped out opinions. She is a grenadier; hard, handsome, manly, inclined to a double chin. She is a pronounced Sapphist and may, thinks Ethel Sands, have an eye on me, old though I am.

VITA Dear Mrs Woolf,

I write this tonight, because I think you said you were going to Spain on the twenty-seventh and I want it to reach you before you go. The PEN Club Committee are very anxious for you to join the club, and at their request I proposed you.

There was a little shout of excitement from the Committee about you, and Galsworthy got up and made a curtsy, so to speak.

VIRGINIA Dear Mrs Nicolson,

But I wish you could be induced to call me Virginia.

VITA My dear Virginia,

You see I don't take much inducing. Could you be induced likewise, do you think?

VIRGINIA Dear Mrs Nicolson,

The secretary of the PEN Club has written to me to say that I have been elected a member. Very regretfully I have had to decline—since I see from the club papers that it is wholly a dining club, and my experience is that I can't belong to dining clubs. But I'm very sorry, as I should like to know the members, and see you also. But this last I hope can be managed in other ways. Could you be persuaded to write a story for the Hogarth Press?

VITA I hope that no-one has ever yet, or ever will, thrown down a glove I was not ready to pick up. On the peaks of Italian mountains, and beside green lakes, I am writing a story for you. I shut my eyes to the blue of gentians. I shut my ears to the brawling of rivers; I shut my nose to the scent of pines; I concentrate on my story, and to you alone, it shall be dedicated. Will you ever play truant to Bloomsbury and culture, I wonder, and come travelling with me? Will you come next year to the place where the Gypsies of all nations make an annual pilgrimage to some Madonna or other? I am going. I think you had much better come too. Look on it, if you like, as copy—as I believe you look upon everything, human relationships included. Oh yes, you like people better through the brain than through the heart. And then, I don't believe one ever knows people in their own surroundings; one only knows them away; divorced from all the little strings and cobwebs of habit. Either *I* am at home, and you are strange; or *you* are at home, and

I am strange; so neither is the real essential person, and confusion results. But in the Basque provinces, among a horde of zingaros, we should both be equally strange and equally real and I think you had better make up your mind to take a holiday and come.

VIRGINIA My dear *Vita*,

I enjoyed your intimate letter from the Dolomites. It gave me a great deal of pain—which is I've no doubt the first stage of intimacy. You say I've "no friends, no heart, only an indifferent head". Nevermind: I enjoyed your abuse very much. But I will not go on else I should write you a really intimate letter, and then you would dislike me, more, even more, than you do.

VITA Aren't you a pig, to make me feel one? I have searched my brain to remember what on earth in my letter could have given you "a great deal of pain". Or was it just one of your phrases, poked at me? Anyhow, that wasn't my intention, as you probably know. Do you ever mean what you say, or say what you mean? Or do you just enjoy baffling the people who try to creep a little nearer? "Dislike you more, even more." Dear Virginia, said she putting her cards on the table, you know very well that I like you a fabulous lot.

VIRGINIA But really and truly you did say—I can't remember exactly what, but to the effect that I made copy out of all my friends, and cared with head, not with the heart. As I say, I forget; and so we'll consider it cancelled!... I like the story very very much—in fact, I began reading it after you left, went out for a walk, thinking of it all the time, and came back and finished it, being full of a particular kind of interest which I daresay has something to do with its being the sort of thing I should like to write myself.

VITA I have walked on air all day since getting your letter. I am more pleased than I can tell you at your approval. Altogether after reading it I felt like a stroked cat.

VIRGINIA "Look on it, if you like, as copy, as I believe you look upon everything, human relationships included". Oh yes, you like people better "through the brain than through the heart", etc: so there. Come and be forgiven.

VITA I came to Tavistock Square today. I went upstairs and rang your bell—I went downstairs and rang your bell. Nothing but dark inhospitable stairs confronted me. So I went away disconsolate. I wanted (a) to see you; (b) to ask you to sign two of your books which my mother had; (c) to be forgiven.

VIRGINIA You have added to your sins by coming here without telephoning—I was only rambling the streets to get a breath of air—could easily have stayed in, wanted very much to see you. I will sign as many books as Lady Sackville wants. No: I will not forgive you. Your book, *Seducers in Equador* looks very pretty, rather like a ladybird. The title however slightly alarms the old gentlemen in Bumpuses Bookshop.

VITA I have been horribly remiss in writing to thank you for *Mrs Dalloway,* but as I didn't want to write you the how-charming-of-you-to-send-me-your-book-I-am-looking-forward-to-reading-it-so-much sort of letter, I thought I would wait until I had read both it and *The Common Reader,* which I am sorry to say I have now done. Sorry, because although I shall read them again, the first excitement of following you along an unknown road is over. There are passages of *The Common Reader* that I should like to know by heart; it is superb; there is no more to be said. I can't think of any book I like better or will reread more often. *Mrs Dalloway* is different; its beauty is in its brilliance chiefly; it bewilders, illuminates, and reveals; *The Common Reader* grows into a guide, philosopher and friend, while *Mrs Dalloway* remains a will-of-the-wisp, a dazzling and lovely acquaintance.

VIRGINIA Hah ha! I thought you wouldn't like *Mrs Dalloway.* On the other hand, I thought you might like *The Common Reader,* and I'm very glad that you do—all the more that it's just been conveyed to me that Logan Pearsall Smith thinks it's "very disappointing". But oh, how one's friends bewilder one!—partly, I suppose, the result of bringing out two books at the same time. I'm trying to bury my head in the sand, or play a game of racing my novel against my criticism according to the opinions of my friends. Sometimes *Mrs Dalloway* wins, sometimes *The Common Reader*. And I have one of my wretched headaches.

VITA Last Friday at midnight I stood on the top of your Downs, and, looking down over various lumps of blackness, tried to guess which valley contained Rodmell and you asleep therein. And now comes your letter, making me think that on the contrary you were probably awake and in pain. But knowing nothing of that at the time, I reluctantly recovered my dogs who had been galloping madly across the Downs, climbed into the motor, and drove through the sleeping villages of Sussex and Kent, with the secret knowledge in my own mind that I had paid you a visit of which you knew nothing, —more romantic than the cup of tea to which your husband, Leonard, had bidden me on Saturday. I have been making a tiny garden of Alpines in an old stone trough, —a real joy. Shall I make an even tinier one for you? In a seed pan, with Lilliputian rocks?

VIRGINIA Tell me who you've been seeing; even if I have never heard of them—that will be all the better. I try to invent you for myself, but find I really have only two twigs and three straws to do it with. I can get the sensation of seeing you—hair, lips, colour, height, even, now and then, the eyes and hands, but I find you going off, to walk in the garden, to play tennis, to dig, to sit smoking and talking, and then I can't invent a thing you say—This proves what I could write reams about—how little we know anyone, only movements and gestures, nothing connected, continuous, profound. But give me a hint I implore.

VITA I am going to Brighton today, over your Downs, and shall leave this letter on your doorstep together with your garden-in-a-saucer. But it will be very tantalizing, stopping at your house. I shan't even ring the bell, and trust to luck that Leonard will fall over the saucer as he goes out.

VIRGINIA Oh you scandalous ruffian! To come as far as this
house and make off! When the cook came up to me with
your letter, and your flowers and your garden, with the
story that a lady had stopped a little boy in the village and
given him them I was so furious I almost sprang after you
in my nightgown.

VITA You are a very, very remarkable person. Of course I always
knew that—it is an easy thing to know—the *Daily Express*
knows it—*The Times* knows it—the *Daily Herald* quotes
you as an authority on the vexed question as to whether
one should cross the road to dine with Wordsworth—but
I feel strongly that I have only tonight thoroughly and
completely realized how remarkable you really are. You
see, you accomplish so much. Yet you give the impression
of having infinite leisure. One comes to see you: you are
prepared to spend two hours of time in talk. One may not,
for reasons of health, come to see you: you write divine
letters. You read bulky manuscripts. You advise on grocers.
You produce books which occupy a permanent place on one's
bedside shelf next to Gerard Manly Hopkins and the Bible.
You cast a beam across the dingy landscape of the *Times
Literary Supplement*. You set up type. You offer to read and
to criticize one's poems,—criticize, meaning illumination,
not complete disheartenment which is the legacy of other
critics. How is it done? I can only suppose that you don't
fritter. Now here am I, alone at midnight, and I survey my
day, and I ask myself what I have done with it. I finished
the hop picking article for Leonard, found an envelope and
a stamp, and sent it off. I planted perhaps a hundred bulbs.
I played tennis with my son, I endeavoured to amuse my
other son, who has whooping-cough, and tries to crack jokes
between the bouts. I read a detective story in my bath. I
talked to a carpenter. I wrote five lines of poetry. Now what
does all that amount to? Nothing. Just fritter. And yet it
represents a better day than I have spent for a long time.

VIRGINIA Do keep it up—your belief that I achieve things. I
assure you, I have need of all your illusions after six weeks

of lying in bed, drinking milk, now and then turning over and answering a letter. We go back on Friday; what have I achieved? Nothing. Hardly a word written, masses of complete trash read, you not seen? The blessed headache goes—I catch a cold or argue violently and it comes back. But now it has gone longer than ever before, so if I can resist the delights of chatter, I shall be robust for ever. But what I was going to say was to ask for more illusions. I can assure you, if you'll make me up, I'll make you up.

VITA I wish that you were well and that I could come and see you. I wrote to you at Rodmell before I knew you were going back to London. You will receive this one before the other. I will therefore conceal from you the destination of my journeying, so that the other letter should not be deprived of its little bit of news. Although news is the last thing one wants or expects to find in letters. I will only tell you that I am not going to the Riviera or Italy, or even Egypt, but some country wild, beautiful and unsophisticated; further away in time, though not in space, than China.

VIRGINIA But for how long? For ever? I am filled with envy and despair. Think of seeing Persia—think of never seeing you again. The doctor has sent me to bed: all writing forbidden. So this is my swan song.

VITA No, not for ever. And not even immediately. Harold goes next month, and I follow in January, to return in May, and then go again next October. So you see there will be a good deal of coming and going. I've evolved some theories about friendship. I think, among other things, that the set hour is full of peril; what one wants is the sudden desultory talk,—the look-up from the book one is reading, the burst of argument between two regions of silence. All this is to invite your attention to the advantages of my country home, Long Barn, as a convalescent home.

VIRGINIA The doctor says I may go away. Would you like me to come to you for a day or two, if you are alone, before the twentieth? I expect this is too late and too difficult; I only suggest it on the off chance.

VITA I would love you to come, as you know.

VIRGINIA Would Tuesday afternoon suit you? Should I stay till Friday or Saturday? Should Leonard come and fetch me back? Should you mind if I only brought one dressing-gown? Should I be a nuisance if I had breakfast in bed?

VITA You can have breakfast, lunch and dinner in bed if you feel like it. Yes, bring a dressing-gown. Yes, let Leonard come whenever he likes. *(To the audience)* I fetched her and brought her down to Long Bam.

Both sit together.

VIRGINIA *(to the audience)* These Sapphists *love* women. Their friendship is never untinged with amorosity. I like her and being with her and the splendour—she shines in the grocer's shop in Sevenoaks with a candlelit radiance, standing on legs like beech trees, pink glowing, grape-clustered, pearl hung. She found me incredibly dowdy.

VITA *(to the audience)* She had got on a new dress. It was very odd indeed, orange and black with a hat to match—a sort of top hat made of straw with two orange feathers, like Mercury's wings—but although odd it was curiously becoming and it pleased Virginia because there could be absolutely no doubt as to which was the front and which was the back.

VIRGINIA *(to the audience)* She said she knew no-one who cared less for personal appearance—no-one put on things the way I did. Yet I was so beautiful, etc. What is the effect of all this on me? Very mixed. There is her maturity and her voluptuousness, her being so much in full sail on high tides, where I am coasting down backwaters; her capacity, I mean, to take the floor in any company, to represent her country, to visit Chatsworth, to control silver, servants, show dogs, her motherhood, her being in short what I have never been, a real woman. And she lavishes on me maternal protection which for some reason is what I've always wanted from everyone.

VITA *(to the audience)* She is an exquisite companion. She's so vulnerable under all that brilliance. I love her dearly but I don't want to get landed in an affair which might get beyond my control. Harold says it would be like smoking over a petrol tank.

VIRGINIA *(to the audience)* I was always sexually cowardly. My terror of real life has always kept me in a nunnery. Clive and now Vita call me a fish and I reply while holding hands and getting exquisite pleasure from contact with either male or female body. But what I want of you is illusion, to make the world dance.

VITA *(to the audience)* I'm scared to death of arousing physical feelings in her because of the madness. I don't know what effect that would have you see, and that is a fire with which I have no wish to play.

VIRGINIA I have left behind a raincoat, a crystal ruler, a diary for the year 1903, a pair of scarlet gloves, a brooch and a hot-water bottle, so contemplate complete nudity by the end of the year. I am very very charming; and Vita is a dear old rough-coated sheep dog. I am dashing off to buy another pair of gloves. Now for a bus down Southampton Row. Ah, but I like being with Vita.

VITA And it's on Wednesday fortnight that I go to Persia. What effect does absence have on you? Does it work like the decreasing charm of your Dog Grizzle, which endears her to you the more? I hope so.

VIRGINIA I have just taken Grizzle to a vet in the Gray's Inn Road. Ah, if you want my love for ever and ever you must break out in spots on your back.

VITA Why does one ever read anybody but Shakespeare? He is coming to Persia with me—the complete works. Such a fuss here. The luggage all plastered with labels. Things scattered all over the room. And my cousin Eddy chattering while I try to remember what I have to pack. "Do you know T. S. Eliot?" No, I don't. Kodak films, aspirin, fur gloves, tooth powder. "Aren't the woodcuts in the *Anatomy of Melancholy* too lovely!" "No, Eddy, I think they are quite awful. —Don't put my riding boots in my suitcase, one doesn't ride on board ship." "Shall I have my sitting-room pink or yellow?" And so on. So is my packing conducted.

VIRGINIA Do not snuff the stinking tallow out of your heart. Poor Virginia to wit and Dog Grizzle.

VITA I am reduced to a thing that wants Virginia. I composed a beautiful letter to you in the sleepless nightmare hours of the night, and it has all gone: I miss you, in a quite simple desperate human way. You would never write so elementary a phrase as that; you'd clothe it in so exquisite a phrase that it would lose a little of its reality. Whereas with me it is quite stark: I miss you even more than I could have believed; and I was prepared to miss you a good deal. So this is just really a squeal of pain.

VIRGINIA But why do you think I don't feel, or that I make phrases? "Lovely phrases", you say, which rob things of reality. Just the opposite. Always, always, always I try to say what I feel. Will you then believe that after you went last Tuesday—exactly a week ago—out I went into the slums of Bloomsbury, to find a barrel organ. But it didn't make me cheerful and ever since, nothing important has happened— somehow it's dull and damp. I have been dull; I have missed you. I do miss you. I shall miss you. And if you don't believe it, you're a long-eared owl and ass. Lovely phrases...? Yes, I miss you, I miss you. I dare not expatiate, because you will say I am not stark, and cannot feel the things dumb people feel. You know that is rather rotten rot, my dear Vita. After all, what is a lovely phrase? One that has mopped up as much truth as it can hold—Also, you'll be so excited, happy and all that. You'll have forgotten me. I'll cut a very poor show against Teheran.

VITA The wish to steal Virginia overcomes me—steal her, take her away, and put her in the sun. You know you liked Greece. You know you liked Spain. Well, then? If I can get myself to Africa and Asia, why can't you?

VIRGINIA I've been awfully worried by elderly relations. Three old gentlemen round about seventy, have discovered that my sister Vanessa is living in sin with Duncan Grant, and that I have written *Mrs Dalloway*—which equals living in sin. Their method of showing their loathing is to come and call, to ask Vanessa if she ever sells a picture, me if I've been in a lunatic asylum lately. Then they intimate how they live in Berkeley Square or the Athenaeum and dine with—I don't know whom: and so take themselves off. It was four weeks yesterday that you went?

VITA We returned from Luxor to Cairo with the train on fire; the dining-car blazing merrily behind us like the tail of a comet. Nobody seemed to mind, the long slim white train pulled up in the night and flames licking out from under the carriage, and a crowd of dark men throwing buckets of water. I talked to the engine driver; a tiny black man in a scarlet turban. He said it was a single line, and that as there was another train due we should probably run into it. He said also that robbers were in the habit of putting boulders on the line, but that he never took any notice of these, but drove full speed at them, lest by pulling up he should be accused of complicity with the robbers. I had a lingering regret for the South-Eastern Railway.

VIRGINIA You are missing the loveliest spring there has ever been in England. We were motored all through Oxfordshire two days ago... The people who took us were Leonard's brother and his wife. I promptly fell in love, not with him or her, but with being stockbrokers, with never having read a book except John Buchan, with not having heard of Roger, or Clive, or Duncan, or Lytton. Oh this is life, I kept saying to myself; and what is Bloomsbury, or Long Barn either, but a contortion, a temporary knot; and why do I pity and deride the human race, when its lot is profoundly peaceful and happy? I extract by degrees a great deal from your letters. They might be longer; they might be more loving. But I see your point—life is too exciting.

VITA I am now at sea. There is a Hindu temple appeared now, on a promontory, and the steerage passengers are casting coconuts into the sea towards it; not so much for the sake of using it as a coconut-shy, but as a mark of respect. Can you imagine coming round the corner from the Coliseum, and seeing Lady Colefax throwing coconuts at St Martin-in-the-Fields.

VIRGINIA I think of you, instead of my novel; I've thought of many million things to tell you. Devil that you are, to vanish to Persia and leave me here! And, dearest Vita, we are having two water-closets made, one paid for by *Mrs Dalloway*, the other by *The Common Reader:* both dedicated to you.

VITA I dined with some super millionaire Americans and found *The Common Reader* in their sitting-room. It gave me a shock. There was your name sprawling on the table. And there was a young American poet there, Archibald MacLeish, who has a passionate admiration for you. You and T. S. Eliot are the only two writers in England today, etc, etc, etc. I don't know whether to be dejected or encouraged when I read the works of Virginia Woolf. Dejected because I shall never be able to write like that, or encouraged because somebody else can? Why is it that critics pay so little attention to style and surface texture? Now you have the *mot juste* more than any modern writer I know. The funny thing is, that you are the only person I have ever known properly who was aloof from the more vulgarly jolly sides of life.

VIRGINIA As for the *mot juste,* you are quite wrong. Style is a very simple matter, it is all rhythm. Once you get that, you can't use the wrong words. But on the other hand here I am sitting after half the morning, crammed with ideas, and visions, and so on, and can't dislodge them, for lack of the right rhythm. Now this is very profound, what rhythm is, and goes far deeper than words. A sight, an emotion, creates this wave in the mind, long before it makes words to fit it; and in writing such is my present belief one has to recapture this, and set this working which has nothing apparently to do with words and then, as it breaks and tumbles in the mind, it makes words to fit it. But no doubt I shall think differently next year. I agree about my lack of jolly vulgarity. But then think how I was brought up! No school; mooning about alone among my father's books; never any chance to pick up all that goes on in schools—throwing balls; ragging; slang; vulgarity; scenes; jealousies—the only rages with my half brothers, and being walked off my legs round the Serpentine by my father. This is an excuse: I am often conscious of the lack of jolly vulgarity, but did Proust pass that way? Did you? Can you chaff a table of officers?

VITA My bringing-up wasn't so very different from yours: I mooned about too, at Knole mostly, and hadn't even a brother or a sister to knock the corners off me. And I never went to school. If I am jolly and vulgar, you can cry quits on another count, for you have that interest in humanity which I can never manage. Now I shall not tell you about Persia, and nothing of its space, colour and beauty, which you must take for granted—but please do take it for granted, because it has become a part of me, —grafted on to me, leaving me permanently enriched. You smile? Well, I have been stuck in a river, crawled between ramparts of snow, been attacked by a bandit, been baked and frozen alternately, travelled alone with men, all strangers, slept in odd places. Eaten wayside meals, crossed high passes, seen Kurds and Medes and caravans, and running streams, and black lambs skipping under blossoms, seen hills of porphyry stained with copper sulphate, snow-mountains in a great circle, endless plains, with flocks on the slopes. Seen a dead camel pecked by vultures, a dying donkey, a dying man. Came to mud towns at nightfall, stayed with odd gruff Scotchmen, drunk Persian wine. Been taken to a party, and introduced to about five hundred English people, five hundred foreign diplomats, and a thousand Persians. Had lunch with the Persian Prime

Minister who has a red beard. Began to stammer in Persian. And today's my birthday. I wish life was three times as long, and every day of it forty-eight hours instead of twenty-four.

VIRGINIA Oh I do miss you; I think of you: I have a million things, not so much to say, as to sink into you.

VITA I have had a letter from you saying you had fallen in love with being a stockbroker—WELL. Just back from the Shah's palace, where I had to go and see the Crown jewels. I am blind. Blinded by diamonds. I have been in Aladdin's cave. I can't talk about it now. It was simply the Arabian Nights, with decor by the Sitwells. Pure fantasy. Oh, why weren't you there?

VIRGINIA I was at a ghastly party at Rose Macaulay's, where in the whirl of meaningless words I thought Mr O' Donovan said The Holy Ghost, whereas he said "The Whole Coast" and I asking "Where is the Holy Ghost?" got the reply "Where ever the sea is". Am I mad, I thought, or is this wit. "The Holy Ghost?" I repeated. "The Whole Coast. "he shouted, and so we went on, in an atmosphere so repellent that it became like the smell of bad cheese, repulsively fascinating until Leonard shook all over, picked up what he took to be Mrs Gould's napkin, and discovered it to be her spare sanitary napkin. Whereupon this tenth-rate literary respectability all gentlemen in white waistcoats, ladies shingled, unsuccessfully shook to its foundations. I kept saying "Vita would love this."

VITA I went to a Persian tea-party. Ravishing women; almond eyes, red lips, babbling like little birds, pulling their veils about them whenever they heard a noise. Completely silly, but oh so lovely! Much better than your stockbrokers. And one old monster of a mother-in-law, hanging over them, like a hawk over a flock of doves. I shall arrive a week after this letter. I will recite Hafiz to you, bring you silks and scents, try to corrupt you in every possible way and make myself generally agreeable. In the meantime I am as we say here your sacrifice.

VIRGINIA Isn't it odd—the effect geography has in the mind! I felt it pathetic when you were going away; as if you were sinking below the verge. Now that you are rising, I'm jolly again. Everybody is longing to see you. Grizzle is in paroxysms.

VITA Plans ever so slightly changed. I'm coming back via Baghdad. I've made friends with a Pharisee who is travelling with me. He is about to become High Priest Designate of all the Pharisees in India; and is hell bent on making the most of his last secular days. I greatly prefer his sister who has olive skin and gazelle eyes—but there it is.

VIRGINIA Yes, Dearest. We all know that Persia is a rose, and you are an Emperor Moth, Bloomsbury is a rotten biscuit, and I'm a weevil. But when are you coming back?

VITA Home to chaos. The cat has five kittens and Pippin has seven puppies but she's very distressed as we've cut off their tails with a carving knife. And every tulip in my garden has been finished off by the wind. If you come now there'll be nothing to see and you'll think me a bad gardener.

VIRGINIA I would like fifteen puppies with their tails chopped off, ten kittens, three turtledoves and a little conversation.

VITA Dearest I don't want to drag you down here for one night, it would be too tiring and unsettling for you.

VIRGINIA I was at a party last night at Edith Sitwell's in honour of Gertrude Stein, massive in blue sprinkled brocade. She sat enthroned on a broken settee, while Edith swam around her stuck about with jewels like a drowned mermaid.

VITA What a dazzling life you do lead—Gertrude Stein and the Sitwells! —you make me feel a bumpkin.

VIRGINIA The Sitwells was a ghastly frost. I put it in to make you feel a bumpkin—and it did, and thus confirmed my view that other people's parties have a mystery and glamour one's own are without. Are you writing poetry? Do tell me what is the difference between that emotion and the prose emotion? What drives you to one and not the other? ...

VITA I don't believe there is any difference between them. It is surely only a question of the different shape words assume in the mind. People think they may mumble inanities which would make them blush if written in good common English, but which they think fit to print if split up into lines. This alone shows that there isn't any real difference. I shall have however, to give up reading your works at dinner, for they are too disturbing. How well you write, though, confound you. When I read you, I feel no-one has ever written English prose before—knocked it about, put it in its place, made it into a servant.

VIRGINIA Yes, I do write damn well sometimes.

VITA I'm sending you one of Pippin's puppies.

VIRGINIA Your puppy has destroyed my skirt, eaten Leonard's proofs, and done such damage as could be done to the carpet—But she is an angel of light. Leonard says seriously she makes him believe in God...and this after she has wetted his floor eight times in one day.

VITA I want you to come and stay the night at Knole with me.

VIRGINIA But why, darling, honourable Mrs Nicolson, insist on Knole? To see me ridiculous.

VITA To take you on the battlements in the moonlight, to storm the ramparts.

VIRGINIA You know you've broken down more ramparts than anyone.

VITA I don't think I've ever wanted anything so much in my life.

VIRGINIA I don't think Knole is possible; for this reason: I tore all my clothes on the gorse, and I can't get any more, and I couldn't ask the butler to wait on me, nor is it for the dignity of letters that I should eat behind a screen, so I don't see how I can come to Knole, all in holes, without a pin to my hair or a stocking to my foot. You'd be ashamed; you'd say things you would regret. I'm partly teasing. I don't mind being dowdy, dirty, shabby, red nosed, middle classed and all the rest. I do want to see you, I do—I do.

VITA There is at the back of my mind a glow, a sort of nebula, which only when I examine it hardens into a shape: "Virginia is coming to Knole on Saturday". But of course she won't, she won't! Something will happen. Something always does, when one wants a thing too passionately. You will have chickenpox, or I shall have mumps, or the house will fall down on Saturday morning. If ever you tried not to have chickenpox, try now. If ever you tried not to be given a headache by Sybil Colefax, try now. I remember, ominously, that you said you were going to tea with her on Friday. Please try with all your might not to let anything happen. It's our last chance before I have to leave England.

VIRGINIA No—I can't come, I have caught eczema from Grizzle. My hair comes out in tufts. I scratch incessantly. It wouldn't be safe for you, or, what matters more, the puppies. I shall think of you: let that console us. That joke being done with, yes, I'll come. It's true I'm incredibly dirty; have washed my head—hair is down, shoes in holes. But d'you know what happened today? I was rushing into a shop to buy a velvet coat, when a woman said, "Any stains to take out?" "Good God," I said, "I have at least twelve on me at the moment." So I bought her ointment, and all my stains are vanished like snow, so life has turned its rosier cheek.

VITA I have a full moon for you. It will be beautiful. I suppose I can manage to exist till Saturday but I'm not sure.

VIRGINIA Yes, it will be nice. Yes, it will. And shall you be very kind to me?

VITA *(to the audience)* We wandered all over the house, pulling up the blinds. She and Dada got on splendidly.

VIRGINIA *(to the audience)* Lord Sackville lives in the kernel of a vast nut. Knole is a conglomeration of buildings half as big as Cambridge. I dare say if you stuck Trinity, Clare and Kings together you might approximate. But the extremities and indeed the inward parts are gone dead.

VITA *(to the audience)* I was cheated at Knole. It should have been mine. Mine. Mine. Mine. We were meant for each other. It is exactly as though for years I had had a liaison with a beautiful woman who never, from force of circumstances belonged to me wholly but who had for me a sort of half maternal tenderness and understanding in which I could be entirely happy. We have been parted through force of circumstances and owing to no choice of her own. She is forced to marry someone else. I can only visit her. But if I were wilder and more ruthless, I should burst in one evening and surprise her.

VIRGINIA *(to the audience)* All these ancestors and centuries and silver and gold have bred a perfect body. She is stag-like or racehorse-like, except for the face which pouts, but as a body hers is perfection.

VITA *(reading from a book)* So in the prison of her perfect shape

She dwelt forever virginal adored

Whence she might never know escape,

Might never know what mystery lay stored

Beyond the threshold she might never pass,

But where forever poised and wavering she was.

Why come Princess for all your grand pretence

You've nothing better in the world to do;

So stay with one who'd change for paltry pence

This hour against the riches of Peru.

Come drop your fan and if you need a screen,

Seek it behind a branch of Myrtle green.

Are you happy? I am.

VIRGINIA Yes. I am entirely and wholly happy.

VITA Beloved Virginia, one last goodbye. I feel torn in a thousand pieces—it is bloody—I can't tell you how I hate leaving you. I don't know how I shall get on without you—in fact I don't feel I can—you have become so essential to me. Bless you for all the happiness you gave me. Put honey when you write.

VIRGINIA Sweet honey. You like to think of me unhappy, I know—well you can. *(To the audience)* And I went home carrying her and Knole in my eyes as I travelled back in the train with the middle classes through the slums. There is Knole capable of housing all the desperate poor of Judd Street and with only that solitary lord in the kernel.

VITA Moscow was gold, green, red, blue roofs above the snow; and the scarlet Soviet flag, lit up from below at night just like the columns of Selfridges, floating over the Kremlin; and all the traffic passing to and fro over the frozen river as though it were a road, and sleighs everywhere, and coachmen stuffed out with straw. I went to visit Lenin. He lies embalmed in a scarlet tomb just below the red flag, and the crowd walks round his glass case two by two. A woman had hysterics just behind me; screamed like an animal; sobbed; screamed again; nobody took any notice—and what do I think of? I think of Virginia in her blue overall, leaning against the doorpost of Tavistock Square, and waving.

VIRGINIA I feel dissipated and aimless. I've settled down to wanting you doggedly, dismally, faithfully. I hope that pleases you. It's damned unpleasant for me, I can assure you. I sit over the gas fire in my sordid room. Why can't I write except in sordid rooms? I don't think I could write a word in your room at Long Barn. And then I'm not writing a novel: this journalism is such a thin, draggled, straining business, and I keep opening the lid and looking into my mind to see whether some slow fish isn't rising there—some new book. No: nothing at the moment.

VITA The moment we had arrived in Persia we began talking about how to get back. Darling, the queerness of human beings strikes me more and more forcibly here. You see, it is just the opposite of London. In London people meet together because some common interests bind them; here, we are just a collection of people thrown together through a purely fortuitous circumstance, with nothing in common except the place we happen to find ourselves in. So that is the one and only topic. I go to call on some bloody Pole or Belgian, and we know that there is nothing to talk about except the Trebizond road, or the Shiraz road, and whether one has done it or not, and whether one is going away for the summer or not, and whether we may expect more snow. There is nothing else, except the cardinal facts of life, and foreign diplomats do not talk about copulation with the same readiness as our friends in England. I should like to see how you would manage it. I said to the clergyman's daughter, how was she liking Teheran? and she replied, "Well, really, the amateur theatricals seem to be the only excitement." Persia, Rheza, the swarming bazaars, Asia—these are not excitements, nor is a civilization thousands of years old, nor the spectacle of a worn-out nation. But Mrs Fairley comes to tea, and Mrs Wilkinson comes to luncheon, and so it's not so bad, and one can always watch the football, and it is possible to get marmalade though it's more expensive than it ought to be, "but I don't like that pomegranate jam, do you?" Meanwhile I cannot write, so am miserable—

VIRGINIA We're still talking, you'll be surprised to hear, about love and sodomy. Then Morgan says he's worked it out and one spends three hours on food, six on sleep, four on work, two on love. Lytton says ten on love. I say the whole day on love. I say it's seeing things through a purple shade. But you've never been in love they say. And I smile and think today's the day I should be trotting out to buy your loaf and watching for your white legs coming down the basement steps. Instead you're on the heights of Persia riding an Arab mare, I daresay, to some deserted garden and picking yellow tulips.

VITA I want to talk to you, just talk and talk and talk and talk. Darling, beloved, Virginia, I can't believe that I was intended for the diplomatic career. Harold unfortunately seems to think that he was. We sit down to dinner. We have too much to eat; too much to drink, sherry, white wine, claret, champagne and liqueurs. After dinner we play poker—at least, the more fortunate among us do; the less fortunate engage in conversation. That is, they talk to people in whom they have no interest about subjects in which they have no interest. And behind it all—just as in Proust, behind the figures of Mme Verdurin and Baron de Charlus lurks the stormy tragedy of Dreyfus and perversion and jealousy,—behind it all lurks the storm-cloud of Russia and conflicting interests, and poor Persia, divided, rotted by disease, poverty and helplessness; and the concupiscence of short-sightedness, and greed of man.

VIRGINIA ...Do you realize how devoted I am to you? There's nothing I wouldn't do for you, dearest honey. It's true, the other night, I did take a glass too much. I got a little tipsy. And then Bobo Mayor is a great seducer in her way. She has Gypsy blood in her: she's rather violent and highly coloured, sinuous too, with a boneless body, and thin hands; all the things I like. So being a little tipsy about twelve o'clock at night, I let her do it. She cut my hair off. I'm shingled, well sort of bobbed. That being so—and it will look all right in a month or two, the hairdresser says, "bound to be a little patchy at first"—let's get on to other things. Mary says it looks quite nice. It's off; it's in the kitchen bucket: my hairpins have been offered up like crutches in St Andrews, Holborn, at the high altar. You shall ruffle my hair in May, honey: it's as short as a partridge's rump.

VITA But are you really shingled? Is it true? Oh darling, do I like that? I think I preferred the dropping hairpins, that cheerful little cascade that used to tinkle on to your plate. But Mary says you look nice shingled, does she? And Mary ought to know.

VIRGINIA I have bought a coil of hair, which I attach by a hook. It falls into the soup, and is fished out on a fork.

VITA It's just as well you did it while I was away, or I should certainly have got the blame. I've just been to dinner with a young Persian—he's in love with me—such a nice creature, he chants Persian poetry beautifully. I wake in the Persian dawn, and say to myself "Virginia, Virginia..."

VIRGINIA Philip Ritchie told me I was the chief coquette in London. *"Allumeuse"* Clive corrected him. Then my suspenders came down, dragging with them an old rag of a chemise. Are you well? Are you drowned? Are you shot? Raped, tired, lost? Lord! I'd give a good deal to know.

VITA I think it's really admirable the way I keep my appointments. I said I would be back on the tenth and here I am, rolling up in London at eleven fifty on the ninth, with ten minutes to spare. It is *marvellous* to be actually in England. Darling, darling, Virginia it's quite incredible to see you.

VIRGINIA We will have a very merry summer: one night perhaps at Long Barn: another at Rodmell: we will write some nice pieces of prose and poetry: we will saunter down the Haymarket. We will *not* dine with Sybil Colefax at Argyll House. We will snore.

ACT II

VIRGINIA Where does one buy a black coat? I have to do a broadcast, and think it should be done in broadcloth.

VITA One buys black *velvet* coats, I don't know about broadcloth, at Debenham & Freebody for twenty-five shillings. Do get one. You'll look nice in it. I have just read the last words of *To The Lighthouse*. I can only say I am dazzled and bewitched. How did you do it? How did you walk along that razor-edge without falling? I wonder if you know how like Mrs Ramsay you are yourself? But perhaps that's because she is your mother. My darling, what a lovely book! I love you more for it.

VIRGINIA I don't know if I'm like Mrs Ramsay. As my mother died when I was thirteen probably it's a child's view of her: but I have some sentimental delight in thinking that you like her. She has haunted me: but then so did that old wretch my father. I was more like him than her, I think; and therefore more critical: but he was an adorable man, and somehow, tremendous. I have to lecture at Oxford. Ask Harold whether one can say that God does not exist to Oxford undergraduates?

VITA Harold says be as rude about God at Oxford as you would be at Cambridge. I thought this absurd photograph would amuse you. Does it?

VIRGINIA Yes, it does amuse me, the picture of you on your donkey, or was it a mule perhaps? That damned chill has landed me with a damned headache, so I am staying in bed.

VITA It was a mule, of course. One rides donkeys at Margate, not on the Persian mountains.

VIRGINIA The Seafarers Educational Society has bought two copies of *To The Lighthouse*. It's an awful thought that the merchant service will be taught navigation by me: will you please be rather strict for a time? It's so easy, with this damned disease, to start a succession of little illnesses, and finally be sent to bed for six weeks.

VITA But when have I ever been anything but "rather strict", except possibly, towards midnight? But that doesn't count. Do you know what I should do, if you were not a person to be rather strict with? I should steal my own motor out of the garage at ten tomorrow night, be at Rodmell by eleven five; throw gravel at your window, then you'd come down and let me in; I'd stay with you till five and be home by half-past six. But, you being you, I can't; more's the pity. Have you ever read my book *Challenge?* I doubt it. It was only published in America. It's the story, thinly disguised, of my affair with Violet Trefusis. Perhaps I sowed all my wild oats then. Yet I don't feel the impulse has left me; no, by God; and for a different Virginia I'd fly to Sussex in the night.

VIRGINIA You see I wired you as I was reading your book *Challenge* and I thought your letter was a challenge if only you weren't so elderly and valetudinarian was what you said in effect we would be spending the night together whereupon I wired "come then" to which naturally there was no answer and a good thing too I daresay as I am elderly and valetudinarian, —it's no good disguising the fact.

VITA Chance missed,—damn. Dottie Wellesley is here and we stayed playing tennis at Sherfield and didn't get home till evening when I found your wire. I could easily have fetched you, but I expect you would have talked more than was good for you. Your friend Edith Sitwell seems to be entering upon a regular campaign; whichever way I turn, that Gorgon's head springs up on my path. I wish you'd draw her out about it next time you see her.

VIRGINIA I think I'm going to see Edith soon—I like her; she's a character.

VITA I am not annoyed, only vastly amused, and rather puzzled; she says my poem *The Land* is "the worst poem in the English language"; now I'm *not* vain, as you know, but I'm hanged if it's as bad as all that!

VIRGINIA I don't think you probably realize how hard it is for the natural innovator as she is, to be fair to the natural traditionalist as you are. It's much easier for you to see her good points than for her to see yours; and then you sell, and she don't—all good reasons why being a Sitwell she should vomit in public.

VITA I have missed you horribly this evening.

VIRGINIA Have you?

VITA Ethel Smyth came to listen to the nightingale. Dottie and I sat with her in the wood for three hours. There were at least half a dozen nightingales. I was proud and delighted. But—she couldn't hear them. The poor old thing is deafer than I knew. I was in despair. I kept saying, "Hush! Listen!" and darkling she listened, cocking her head on one side, but never a note could she hear. Then one suddenly burst out in a thorn bush not ten yards away. She heard that all right; and it sang, Virginia, that blessed little bird, it sang for a solid hour, and she was enraptured. So Long Barn and the evening were a great success: "Beloved Vita, call me Ethel", all thanks to the nightingale.

VIRGINIA What am I to do about powder? I'm having lunch with Ethel and she will take it ill if I don't powder my nose. I'll rise to powder but not rouge. I'll leave that to Lady Wellesley.

VITA You must do me credit with Ethel, and without powder or with the wrong sort you certainly wouldn't do me credit. So I telephoned to the chemist and said it must be sent at once.

VIRGINIA You be a careful dolphin in your gambolling on misty moonlight nights or you'll find Virginia's soft crevices lined with hooks.

VITA Dottie Wellesley has just handed me her letter to you, to read. I am shocked. I am seldom shocked, but this time I am. I've told her that in spite of her investing money in the Hogarth Press, you won't be seduced by her. And that you belong to me. But I am afraid she seems to think that doesn't matter. She is sticking up the envelope and sending it all the same.

VIRGINIA Well it's all settled. Lady Dottie Wellesley has bought me. She bailed us out. She paid twenty-five thousand down for the Hogarth Press, so I'm hers for life. I have the use of the Rolls Royce and wine to taste. Speaking sober prose, however, I won't belong to the two of you, or to the one of you, if the two of us belong to the one. In short, if Dottie's yours, I'm not. A profound truth is involved which I leave you to discover. It is too hot to argue: and I am too depressed.

VITA Don't go right away from me. I depend on you more than you know.

VIRGINIA I can't write. I'm rather melancholy.

VITA My darling, why melancholy?

VIRGINIA Circumstances.

VITA I would never break out if you were here but you leave me unguarded.

VIRGINIA I can't speak. Who might be behind the screen.

VITA I wish I were with you today.

VIRGINIA *doesn't answer.*

Damn it I want to know what's the matter.

VIRGINIA Yesterday morning I was in despair—I couldn't screw a word from me; and at last dropped my head in my hands: dipped my pen in the ink, and wrote these words, as if automatically, on a clean sheet: "Orlando: A Biography". No sooner had I done this than my body was flooded with rapture and my brain with ideas. I wrote rapidly till twelve. But listen; suppose Orlando turns out to be Vita: and it's all about you and the lusts of your flesh and the lure of your mind—heart you have none—who go gallivanting down the lanes with Dottie Wellesley or is it Mary Campbell now? Shall you mind?

VITA Mind?

VIRGINIA Say yes, or no.

VITA My God, Virginia, if ever I was thrilled and terrified it is at the prospect of being projected in the shape of Orlando. You see, any vengeance that you ever want to take will lie ready to your hand. You have my full permission. Only I think that having drawn and quartered me, unwound and retwisted me, or whatever it is that you intend to do, you ought to dedicate it to your victim.

VIRGINIA *Orlando* will be a little book, with pictures and a map or two. I make it up in bed at night, as I walk the streets, everywhere. In fact, I have never more wanted to see you than I do now—just to sit and look at you, and get you to talk, and then rapidly and secretly, correct certain doubtful points. About your teeth now and your temper. Is it true you grind your teeth at night? What and when was your moment of greatest disillusionment? If you've given yourself to Mary Campbell, I'll have no more to do with you, and so it shall be written, plainly, for all the world to read in *Orlando*.

VITA Please don't be angry about Mary. It's all such a mess here. Roy Campbell is always drunk and talks of murder and suicide. He has said terrible things to me. I feel suddenly the whole of my life is a failure in so far as I'm incapable of creating one single perfect relationship. What shall I do, Virginia?

VIRGINIA It's just that you can't help attracting the flounderers and it is their second-rateness which is the beginning of my alienation. I can't have it said "Vita's great friends, Dottie, Mary and Virginia". I detest the second-rate schoolgirl atmosphere.

VITA My darling, you were quite right; you have given me a pull-up; I drift too easily. I don't exaggerate when I say that I don't know what I should do if you ceased to be fond of me.

VIRGINIA I'm half, or tenth-part jealous, when I see you with the Marys, and Dotties, and Valeries, and Hildas, so you can discount that. I'm happy to think you do care: for often I seem old, fretful, querulous, difficult tho' charming and begin to doubt. Should you say, if I rang you up to ask, that you were fond of me? If I saw you would you kiss me? If I were in bed would you—I'm rather excited about *Orlando* tonight: have been lying by the fire and making up the last chapter.

VITA If only you'd come before I go to Berlin, all your questions shall be answered in the affirmative. Rebecca West wrote an article about *The Land* which succeeded in annoying me; I resent being told that my feeling for the country is not genuine, but only what I think people *ought* to feel about the country; this is *not* true.

VIRGINIA Damn Rebecca—who doesn't know a poem from a potato.

VITA Berlin is a bloody place, to be sure; and Harold is posted here for three years and my feelings, which if I gave way to them would be all rebellion and despair, —are complicated by the fact that I mustn't hate Berlin because of Harold. That is, it is an implied criticism of him, and a resentment, and I can't bear to harbour any thought which reflects on him—it is all very difficult. The officials charged with preparing the reception of the Afghans were thrown into an agitation, as they were warned that the King of Afghanistan wanted five beds in his room. Was he, then, they asked, bringing four wives? No, he was only bringing one wife, and one lady who for European purposes was to be known as his sister-in-law. Why, then, five beds? Why not three? It then transpired that according to Afghan custom, the remainder of the night may not be spent in any bed in which the act of love has been consummated; therefore, if the King felt inclined to commit that act with either, or both, of the ladies, there must be two spare beds for them to change over into. The Germans thought this very odd. I on the contrary think it reveals a high state of civilization. Do you think that Queen Mary is at this moment supervising the installation of five beds in a bedroom at Buckingham Palace? I haven't heard a word from you. Have you forgotten me? or are you just busy?

VIRGINIA I fell in love with Noël Coward and he's coming to tea. You can't have all the love in Chelsea. I must have some. Noël Coward must have some.

VITA I was not meant to be an Excellency. I feel that the next person who kisses my hand will get his face smacked. I think a lot about Virginia. *Orlando,* I am glad to reflect, compels you willy-nilly to spend a certain amount of your time with me.

VIRGINIA *Orlando* is finished! Did you feel a sort of tug, as if your neck was being broken on Saturday last at five minutes to one? That was when he died—or rather stopped talking, with three little dots... Now every word will have to be re-written, and I see no chance of finishing it by September—It is all over the place, incoherent, intolerable, impossible—And I am sick of it. The question now is, will my feelings for you be changed? I've lived in you all these months—coming out, what are you really like? Do you exist? Or have I made you up?

VITA "Do I exist, or have you made me up?" I always foresaw that, when you had killed Orlando off. Well, I'll tell you one thing: if you like, —no, love me one trifle less now that Orlando is dead, you shall never never set eyes on me again, except by chance at one of Sibyl's parties. I won't be fictitious. I won't be loved solely in an astral body, or in Virginia's world. So write quickly and say I'm still real. I feel terribly real just now—all cockles and mussels, alive alive-oh. Will you come and stay with me when I come home?

VIRGINIA Are you back? At Long Barn? With the dogs? Comfortable? Well? I read in *The Times* that I had won the most insignificant and ridiculous of prizes but I have heard nothing more; so it may be untrue. I don't mind— you'll laugh either way.

VITA I won another prize the other day—I forgot to tell you—in America, but it was only a vast anthology of American verse. I had hoped for dollars.

VIRGINIA I rang you up just now, to find you were gone nutting in the woods with Mary Campbell, or Mary Carmichael, or Mary Seton but not me—damn you...

VITA The nights are marvellous. Full moon, nightingales, and all that business. But where is Virginia? What about Virginia coming here for a night before the moon begins to wane. I *do* want to see you.

VIRGINIA *(to the audience)* Such opulence and freedom, flowers all out, butler, silver, dogs, biscuits, wine, hot water, log fires, Italian cabinets, Persian rugs, books. It's like stepping into a rolling gay sea with nicely crested waves. Yet I like Rodmell better perhaps; more effort and life in it to my mind. Vita very opulent in her brown velvet jacket, pearl necklace and slightly furred cheeks. Her real claim to consideration is, if I may be so coarse, her legs. Oh they are exquisite, running like slender pillars up into her trunk which is that of a breastless Cuirassier. All about her is savage, patrician. If I were she I would merely strike with eleven Elk hounds behind me, through my ancestral woods. And why she writes which she does with complete competence and a pen of brass is a puzzle to me.

VITA I think about my novel. Is it better to be extremely ambitious, or rather modest? Probably the latter is safer; but I *hate* safety, and I would rather fail gloriously than dingily succeed.

VIRGINIA I believe that the main thing in beginning a novel is to feel, not that you can write it, but that it exists on the far side of a gulf which words can't cross; that it's to be pulled through only in a breathless anguish. Now when I sit down to an article, I have a net of words which will come down on the idea certainly in an hour or so. But a novel, as I say, to be good should seem, before one writes it, something unwriteable, only visible; so that for nine months one lives in despair, and only when one has forgotten what one meant, does the book seem tolerable. I assure you, all my novels were first rate before they were written. But you know there's something obscure in you. Something that doesn't vibrate. Something reserved, muted. It's in your writing too. The thing I call central transparency fails you there too.

VITA Damn you, Virginia, you can be devilishly shrewd. I feel very violently about the banning of *The Well of Loneliness*. Not because of my sympathy with the subject; not because I think it is a good book; but really on principle. Because, you see, even if it had been a good book—even if it had been a great book—it still would have been banned because of the lesbianism. And that is intolerable. If only I wasn't back in bloody Berlin. Are you and Leonard really going to get up a protest? Or is it fizzling out? What a conceited ass Radcliffe Hall must be. All the same, don't let it fizzle out. If you got Arnold Bennett and suchlike, it would be bound to make an impression. Avoid Shaw, though: I nearly blew up over the various articles in the *New Statesman*. Personally, I should like to renounce my nationality, as a gesture; but I don't want to become a German, even though I did go to a revue last night in which two ravishing young women sang a frankly lesbian song. Now about your coming to France with me when I get back. I will leave you to your own fluctuations, I will only say, you mustn't come if it's going to make you miserable all the time. But you wouldn't be.

VIRGINIA Suppose we leave on Saturday the twenty-second—Do you want to go second or first?

VITA Either. I am absolutely overjoyed.

VIRGINIA I insist on first on the boat? If first is much more comfortable on the train then first is advisable. Not otherwise; because first-class passengers are always old fat and testy and smell of eau-de-cologne, which makes me sick.

VITA I beg you to get the tickets before you have time to change your mind.

VIRGINIA *(to the audience)* I am alarmed at the thought of a week alone with Vita. We might find each other out.

VITA *(to the audience)* As it was, Virginia fretted because she hadn't heard from Leonard and I worried in case Virginia was overtired. We spent our first evening drinking at the Brasserie Létitia in the rue de Sèvres, writing to our respective husbands on the torn out fly leaves of our respective books. Virginia admitted she and Leonard had had a small but sudden row that morning about her going abroad with me.

VIRGINIA *(to the audience)* We went to a fair at Saulieu and I bought Leonard a green corduroy coat. Then we sat in a field and wrote again to our husbands.

VITA *(to the audience)* It's all very nice. I feel amused and irresponsible. I can talk about life and literature to my heart's content.

VIRGINIA *(to the audience)* I don't think I could stand more than a week away from Leonard as there are so many things to say to him which I can't say to Vita, though she has a heart of gold and a mind which if slow works doggedly and has its moments of lucidity.

VITA Burgundy seems a dream. "Before, a joy proposed; behind a dream." I was very happy. Were you? It is a quarter to one, —nearly two hours after Virginia's bedtime. My dearest, I do love you. All the Sibyls and Tom Eliots in the world don't love you as much as I do.

VIRGINIA It was a very, very nice letter you wrote by the light of the stars at midnight. Always write then, for your heart requires moonlight to deliquesce it. And mine is fried in gaslight, as it's only nine o'clock and I must go to bed at eleven. And so I shan't say anything: not a word of the balm to my anguish—for I am always anguished—that you were to me. How I watched you! How I felt—now what was it like? Well, somewhere I have seen a little ball kept bubbling up and down on the spray of a fountain: the fountain is you; the ball me. It is a sensation I get only from you. It is physically stimulating and restful at the same time.

VITA I was in a bookshop in London yesterday and the bookseller said to me knowingly, "I saw an advance copy of *Orlando*." You will send me a copy?

VIRGINIA I've sent you one.

VITA I need hardly say that I can hardly exist till I get it.

VIRGINIA Do you mind? Say yes, or no.

VITA I am in no fit state to write to you—and as for cold and considered opinions, as you said on the telephone, such things do not exist in such a connection. At least, not yet. For the moment, I can't say anything except that I am completely dazzled, bewitched, enchanted, under a spell. It seems to me the loveliest, wisest, *richest* book that I have ever read, —excelling even your own "Lighthouse". Virginia, I really don't know what to say, —am I right? Am I wrong? Am I prejudiced? Am I in my senses or not? I feel like one of those wax figures in a shop window, on which you have hung a robe stitched with jewels. How could you have hung so splendid a garment on so poor a peg. Really this isn't false humility; *really* it isn't. Also you have invented a new form of Narcissism, —I confess, —I am in love with *Orlando*—this is a complication I had not foreseen.

VIRGINIA What an immense relief! It struck me suddenly with horror that you'd be hurt or angry, and I didn't dare open the post: now let who will bark or bite. Sales much better. Enthusiasm in the *Birmingham Post*. Knole is discovered. They hint at you.

VITA I simply can't bear you to be ill. Do be good and strong minded and don't be social or I'll have to scold you. Although

I am all for the kennel with a little wire run I don't like it to be for that reason; would rather have Virginia well and naughty, than Virginia ill and good. Much, much rather.

VIRGINIA I'm still in bed—no pain for two days and no sleeping draughts, only Bromide. I feel much brighter and clearer and less inclined to curse God for having made such a crazy apparatus as my nervous system. Is it worth it?

VITA Do you know what I believe it was? It was suppressed randiness. I have discovered a bookstall here in Berlin, which deals entirely in homosexual literature, which sounds even funnier in German than it does in English. We went to the sodomites' ball. A lot of them were dressed as women, but I fancy I was the only genuine article. What about a few days at Long Barn when I return? I'll look after you like the most expensive of Scotch nannies with a new baby to powder.

VIRGINIA Do NOT ask Dottie. This I feel strongly about. Twice lately she has utterly ruined my serenity with you; and I won't have it. Choose between us, Lady Dottie Wellesley if your taste inclines that way by all means; but not the two of us in one cocktail.

VITA Darling, it's so complicated.

VIRGINIA Then I'll make it simple. I won't come.

VITA My own fault, no doubt. And am I ever going to see Virginia again? A despair has settled down upon me about it. How does one write a novel? I have come to the conclusion that I am a good walker but a bad novelist. This is perhaps not what you call an intimate letter? But I disagree. The book that one is writing at the moment is really the most intimate part of one, and the part about which one preserves the strictest secrecy. What is love or sex, compared with the intensity of the life one leads *in* one's book?

VIRGINIA I have only one passion in life—cooking. I have just bought a superb oil stove. I can cook anything. I am free forever of cooks. I cooked veal cutlets and cake today. I assure you it is better than writing these more than idiotic books—Well, God knows when we shall meet. You'll be off to America...

VITA We got to Denver, at the foot of the Rockies, and by breakfast time we were climbing right up into the mountains and are now some seven thousand feet up. It is very beautiful, very desolate, the sun is hot, and I've seen a cowboy.

VIRGINIA Shall you net anything after all—with the dollar collapsed? —There'll be the experience, as they call it—all those virgins you've ravished—teas you've eaten, shrines you've visited, fat old women you've intoxicated—I hope California will have stopped quaking by the time you get there. Please, Vita darling, come back soon. Please come snuffing up my stairs soon, just the same, in your red jersey. Please wear your pearls. And will you ask me to your Castle at Sissinghurst. Because you know you love now several people, women I mean, physically I mean, better, oftener, more carnally than me. Write to me.

VITA I've been trying to write to you for days and days, but we're still travelling. I never realized the size of this darn country until we got here. I am now in the middle of the desert with nothing but a few cowboys and a stray coyote to interrupt. Magnificent stars overhead, and mountains all round. The desert itself is carpeted with rosy verbena. It is exactly like Persia, and we are as happy as larks. Los Angeles was hell. Take Peacehaven, multiply it by four hundred square miles, sprinkle it all along the French Riviera, and then empty the Chelsea Flower Show over it, adding a number of Spanish buildings, and you have the Los Angeles coast. Hollywood, however, is fun—pure fantasy—you never know what you'll come upon when you come around the corner, whether half an ocean liner, or Trafalgar Square, or a street in Stratford-on-Avon, with Malayan Houris walking down it. We were taken around by Mr Gary Cooper. Then I saw Elsa Maxwell and the loveliest fish in the aquarium. I doubt if I'll ever recover from all this. At any rate, it's certain that I'll never be the same again. From here we go to Arizona and then to New Mexico, and then to Milwaukee, and then to

South Carolina, and then to New York, and then to that
blessed boat which will bring us home. Battered and
enriched—not only by dollars.

VIRGINIA You're back—When shall I see you? —Suggest any
time, which I'll keep even if it means murder. Lord, how I
envy you the pink tower after all America.

VITA Yes, Sissinghurst was very nice, but I've only had one
day—Saturday—at home so far. So much to do, I don't know
when I am going to see Virginia.

VIRGINIA Last night Jack Hutchinson said "I saw Vita lunching
at the Café Royal today". Oh such a pang of rage shot through
me! All through dinner, and the supper. And it burnt a hole
in my mind, that you should have been lunching at the Café
Royal and not come to see me. How pleased you'll be. And
did it on purpose I daresay. But who were you with? You
knew I should get wind of it—yes, and it was a woman you
were lunching with, and there was I, sitting alone and and
and... Dearest Creature, do write and tell me who you were
lunching with at the Café Royal—and I sitting alone over
the fire—! Oh the Café Royal! When Jack said that, not
to me, but to the company, you could have seen my hand
tremble; and then we all went on talking and the candles
were lit, and I choose mine, a green one, and it was the
first one to die, which means they say that out of the eight
or nine people there, I shall be the first to wear a winding
sheet. But you'll be lunching at the Café Royal!

VITA My lunch at the Café Royal! Well, I was taking Gwen
St Aubyn to a nursing home, and took her to have some
luncheon there first. We didn't then know if she had to
have her head cut open or not. Thank goodness, it turns
out to be not. I can't tell you how gratified I am by your
annoyance on discovering me in unknown company at the
Café Royal—but if I hadn't been on so grim a mission you
may be sure I should have let you know.

VIRGINIA Why has everybody got a book of your poems and
not I? Didn't I give you *Flush* and *Orlando!* Aren't I a critic

too—aren't I a woman? Don't you care what I say? Am I nothing to you, physically morally or intellectually? Look here, Vita, you may be putting off humanity and rising, like the day star,—but do let your last act, in the guise of humanity, be to pack a book, called *V. Sackville West Collected Poems* and sign it for me...

VITA Do you know, it was my native modesty which prevented me from sending you my book. I couldn't believe you really wanted it.

VIRGINIA And the book came. And it's dedicated to Dottie Wellesley. And I've read one or two of the new poems. And I like them—yes I like the one to Enid Bagnold; and I think I see how you may develop differently. You're an odd mixture as a poet. I like you for being "outmoded" and not caring a damn: that's why you're free to change.

VITA I've got eight Alsatian puppies—five weeks old—does Leonard want one, or are Sally's puppies too imminent for him to contemplate any others?

VIRGINIA No: no: what have we spent the last days doing? Rigging up a lying-in bed in Leonard's study; the event comes off this Sunday. Thus we can't go to Rodmell. Dogs enough; if dogs there be. Some say she's still a virgin.

VITA Virginia darling I am sick with anger. Mother has told Ben, my Ben, that his father has had boys in all cities where he has been *en poste,* every detail of my affair with Violet Trefusis and that the marriage was nearly wrecked a second time by you.

VIRGINIA The old woman should be shot.

VITA Not that I'm ashamed of my morals or Harold's.

VIRGINIA No but when one is eighteen words, news, revelations about one's parents have immeasurable force; and that she should have taken it on herself to say them... It seems so dastardly, so immoral, so fiendishly inhuman.

VITA You're an angel to understand so unfailingly when one really minds about something. Ben might have had a horrid imprint sealed on his mind. Luckily he didn't—a tribute, I think, that he could accept without wincing the revelation that his mother and father are both to be numbered with the outcasts of the human race.

VIRGINIA I wired you because Vanessa's son Julian was killed yesterday fighting in Spain. Nessa likes to have me and so I'm round there most of the time. It is very terrible. You'll understand.

VITA I am so terribly sorry. Darling Virginia—I wish I could do or even say something. You are so very dear to me, and you are unhappy—and I can do nothing, except be your ever very loving Vita.

VIRGINIA I've been round with Nessa all day. It has been an incredible nightmare. We had both been certain he would be killed, and the strain on her is now, perhaps mercifully, making her so exhausted she can only stay in bed... Lord why do these things happen? I'm not clear enough in the head to feel anything but varieties of dull anger and despair.

VITA I had a note from Vanessa which ends thus: "I cannot ever say how Virginia has helped me. Perhaps, some day, not now, you will be able to tell her it's true".

VIRGINIA Isn't it odd? Nessa's saying that to you, I mean, meant something I can't speak of. And I can't tell anyone—but I think you guess—how terrible it is to me, watching her: if I could do anything—sometimes I feel hopeless. But that message gives me something to hold to. My book *Three Guineas* comes out tomorrow. It's only a piece of donkey-drudgery, and as it repeats in still soberer prose the theme of that very sober piece *The Years,* which, rightly, you didn't like, I hadn't meant to send it. But I will, by way of thanks, and you need neither read it nor write and say you have. Both books are now off my mind, thank God. Why did I feel I must write them, Lord knows.

VITA You are a tantalizing writer, because at one moment you enchant one with your lovely prose and next moment exasperate one with your misleading arguments. You see, so provocative a book denouncing war can't be thanked for in a mere letter; it would need a reply as long as the book itself. And far be it from me to cross swords with you, for I should always lose on points in fencing, though if it came to fisticuffs I might knock you down. So long as you play the gentleman's game, with the gentleman's technique, you win—I am not explaining myself very well, indeed very badly and confusedly, so shall we leave it till we meet? In the meantime, let me say that I read you with delight, even though I wanted to exclaim, "Oh, BUT, Virginia..." on fifty per cent of your pages.

VIRGINIA Of course I knew you wouldn't like *Three Guineas*— that's why I wouldn't, unless you had sent a postcard with a question, have given it you. All the same, I don't quite understand. You say you don't agree with fifty per cent of it—no, of course you don't. But when you say that you are exasperated by my "misleading arguments" — then I ask, what do you mean? If I said, "I don't agree with your conception of Joan of Arc's character", that's one thing. But if I said, "your arguments about her are misleading", shouldn't I mean, "Vita has cooked the facts in a dishonest way in order to produce an effect which she knows to be untrue?" If *that's* what you mean by "misleading" then we shall have to have the matter out, whether with swords or fisticuffs. And I don't think *whichever we use,* you will, as you say, knock me down. It may be a silly book, and I don't agree that it's a well-written book; but it's certainly an honest book: and I took more pains to get up the facts and state them plainly than I ever took with any thing in my life... You say I am curiously feminist. Feminist is a vicious word that has done much harm in its day. Its day I hope is over and men and women will fight together against tyranny. Leonard says you have sent a poem, and would like to know what I think of it. Now I would like to read it and normally would fire off an opinion with my usual audacity. But I want to explain: constituted as I am not as I ought to be I feel I can't read your poem impartially while your charges against me remain unsubstantiated.

VITA But my darling Virginia, never in my life have I ever suspected you of humbug or dishonesty! I was absolutely appalled by your letter this morning. I cannot now remember exactly how I expressed myself in it, but it was to the effect that I had never for a moment questioned your facts or their accuracy in *Three Guineas*, but only disagreed in some places with the deductions you drew from them. And this, after all, is a matter of opinion, not of fact. But my unfortunate allusion to the elegance of your style I meant that you almost succeeded in convincing one in spite of oneself. You know there are few people in the world whom I should hate to hurt more than you, and few people whose integrity I respect or trust more. That you should feel you can't read my poem because of some barrier between us shows me that I must have hurt you. I must have expressed myself clumsily. Your very contrite and entirely devoted Vita.

VIRGINIA What on earth can I have said in my letter to call forth this telegram? God knows. I scribbled it off in five minutes, never read it through, and can only remember that it was written in a vein of obvious humorous extravagance and in a tearing hurry. But, as I say, let's leave it: and I apologize and will never write a letter so carelessly again. And I've no grievance whatever; and you need say no more, because I'm quite sure, on re-reading your letter, you didn't mean that I was dishonest: and that's the only thing I minded. So forgive and forget.

VITA I am asking my publisher to give you a copy of *Solitude* from me. I do wonder what you will think of it, —not much, probably.

VIRGINIA Yes, your publisher has handed me a copy of your book: which I certainly consider my due, with an inscription. I don't believe you care a damn what I think of it. So yesterday Franco was recognized. Julian killed for this. That ridiculous little man Hitler now has more than a million men now under arms.

VITA Harold said yesterday's meeting of the House of Commons was glum in the extreme. Chamberlain like a coroner summing up a murder case.

VIRGINIA War is inevitable I suppose. Not tomorrow but nearer.

VITA Harold has to fly to Egypt. Damn damn damn. I wish flying had never been invented. I shan't have a restful moment till he gets back.

VIRGINIA Leonard says he's taught himself not to think about it—death. Although we have a lethal dose of morphine for suicide should Hitler invade England. No doubt we would be marked down, he as a Jew; both of us as anti-fascists. I shouldn't want to live if he died.

VITA If we are invaded, I would take Dada's guns to the top of the tower and shoot as many Germans as possible before shooting myself.

VIRGINIA Leonard's monkey, Mitzi, died in the night. It was very touching—her eyes shut and her face white like a very old woman's. Leonard had taken her to sleep in his room, and she climbed on to his foot last thing. But enough—don't die—

VITA I was deeply distressed for Leonard on hearing of the death of Mitzi. Please give him my sympathy and tell him he'd better acquire a lemur as soon as possible—they are the most enchanting pets and said to be more allied to the human race than any other animal.

VIRGINIA I've been walking on the marsh and found a swan sitting on a Saxon grave. This made me think of you. Then I came back and read about Leonardo—Kenneth Clark—good I think: this made me also think of you. And in a minute I must cook some macaroni. What is the phrase I always remember? or forget: "look your last on all things lovely".

Sirens.

VITA I find one's war psychology very strange—don't you? Up to twelve o'clock noonday I am the complete coward, dreading air-raids, bombs, gas, et cetera then after twelve noonday I become all brave and British again—and remain brave until the next morning—when the whole thing starts up again in its terrifying cycle of fear, dread and shrinking cowardice. I think you are much braver than I am; or should I call it more philosophical?

VIRGINIA But I don't think I'm philosophic—rather, numbed. Of course I'm not in the least patriotic, which may be a help, and not afraid, I mean for my own body. But that's an old body and I think of death as a great excitement, something active—the one experience I will never describe. I shall go down with my colours flying. Your friendship is a great comfort in this intolerable suspension of all reality— something real.

VITA I find that there are few people these days who give me any sense of real contact, but you certainly do; I suppose one sorrow sifts out the rest.

VIRGINIA A battle against depression today. Routed by clearing out the kitchen. Dearest do come and see me—in fact isn't it a duty in this frozen time to meet as often as possible? So that even in the cold night watches when all the skeletons clank we may keep each other warm.

VITA Everything is so uncertain here with the threat of invasion that I hesitate to suggest a night with you. I'm still "keeping the brave British smile" as the *Daily Sketch* calls it but I wonder how long we shall keep it up? On the top layer I mind what you call the incessant bother of small arrangements, —no physical solitude; the Army here yesterday wanting to use Sissinghurst as their headquarters. Great lorries arriving, gun encasements on the river, evacuees arriving. Seemingly dozens of people to every meal; food rationing, petrol rationing, having to black out windows; having my mother-in-law to stay here for God knows how long; never knowing who is coming or going; people sleeping on sofas— the whole house upside down. Then, underneath this, on the second layer, come the anxieties, the young men one cares about whose lives are upset and who are probably going to lose them in a horrible manner, Ben with an anti-aircraft battery, Nigel waiting, waiting, to be called up into the Guards; Piers aged eighteen already with the artillery; John, my nephew, aged twenty waiting to be called up at any moment. Then on the third layer, deepest of all, comes one's own grief and despair at the wicked folly of it all—I have never felt so tired—physically and spiritually—in all my life.

VIRGINIA Yes, I sit in a dumb rage at being fought for by these children whom one wants to see making love to each other. Dearest creature, how I go on seeing you, tormented. What anguish it is at this time to have sons. How I long to hear from your own lips what's been worrying you—for you'll never shake me off—not for a moment do I feel ever less attached. Ain't it odd? Yes, do, do come and see me. What fun, what joy that will be.

Sounds of a plane passing overhead, then a bomb exploding.

I'd just put flowers in your room when the raid started... Oh! Vita, I can't bear it. What can one say—except that I love you. Dearest—You have given me such happiness.

VITA Oh dear, how your letter touched me this morning. I nearly dropped a tear into my poached egg. I love you too; you know that.

VIRGINIA Do you remember once sitting at Kew Gardens in a purple storm?

VITA I don't like being cut off from you. But you must stay there at Rodmell. I'm sending you something of my own making.

VIRGINIA All I can say is that when we discovered the butter in the post box we called in the whole household—Louie that is—to look. "That's a whole pound of butter," I said. Saying which I broke off a lump and ate it pure. Then in the glory of my heart I gave all our week's ration—which is about the size of my thumb nail—to Louie—earned undying gratitude; then sat down and ate bread and butter. It would have been desecration to add jam. Bombs fell near me: trifles; a plane shot down in the marsh: trifles; floods damned—no, nothing seems to make a fitting wreath for the pedestal holding your butter. Oh, Vita, what a Cornucopia of Bounty you are!

VITA I have never sent you the promised fire lighter. But here it is. The fire lighter is known in America as the Little Wonder and indeed deserves the name.

VIRGINIA There you must stop. You can't add anything to fire. You must see the poetic fitness of ending there.

VITA Another raid on London last night. Oxford Street now smashed, John Lewis, Selfridges, Bourne and Hollingsworth, most of Jermyn Street, and part of the British Museum.

VIRGINIA I ought to go up and see what's left of our house—though there's a sort of relief in losing possessions. I should like to start life in peace—almost bare, free to go anywhere.

VITA Darling, it would be folly to go to London. It's ghastly. Craters everywhere. I went up yesterday. I had a strange *à la recherche du temps perdu* luncheon with Violet Trefusis. She asked me what's known as a leading question about you and me. My birds have died. I couldn't get the right feed.

VIRGINIA Louie's birds survive: and she feeds them on scraps—I suppose they're lower-class humble birds. Do they die all in an instant? What did you say when Violet Trefusis asked you that leading question? I still remember her, like a foxcub, all scent and seduction. Now why did you love her? And did you love Hilda? You swore you didn't that summer... and what about Mary...?

VITA I've just had a terrible shock. Virginia's killed herself. Leonard came home to find a note saying she was going to commit suicide and she drowned herself. If only I'd been there.

Pause.

That lovely mind. That lovely spirit.

Pause.

Some years later I was asked to compile an anthology of poems and I wanted to include one by Virginia. So I took a passage from *Orlando* and split it up into lines.

She begins to recite.

Let us go, then, exploring

This summer morning.

When all are adoring

The plum blossom and the bee.

And humming and hawing.

VIRGINIA *joins in.*

VITA	} Let us ask of the starling
VIRGINIA	} What he may think
	On the brink

VITA *stops and* **VIRGINIA** *finishes the poem.*

VIRGINIA Of the dustbin whence he picks

Among the sticks

Combings of scullion's hair.

What's life we ask;

Life Life Life! cries the bird

As if he had heard.

Curtain.

FURNITURE AND PROPERTY LIST

ACT I

On stage: 2 chairs
Book

ACT II

On stage: As previous ACT

LIGHTING PLOT

Property fittings required: nil
The same scene throughout

ACT I

To open: Full general lighting

No cues.

ACT II

To open: Full general lighting

No cues.

EFFECTS PLOT

ACT I

No cues.

ACT II

Cue 1   **Virginia**: "...on all things lovely."   (Page 41)
                Sirens.

Cue 2   **Virginia**: "What fun, what joy that
                will be."   (Page 43)
                *Airplane overhead, followed by bomb
                  exploding.*

THIS
IS
NOT
THE
END

Printed in the USA
CPSIA information can be obtained
at www.ICGtesting.com
LVHW011319270823
756411LV00011B/953